MY FIRST

# PRESIDENTS' DAY BOOK

by Aileen Fisher
illustrated by Lydia Halverson

created by The Child's World

 CHILDRENS PRESS ®
CHICAGO

**Library of Congress Cataloging in Publication Data**

Fisher, Aileen Lucia.
    My first Presidents' Day book.

    Summary: Recounts in verse some highlights from the
lives of George Washington and Abraham Lincoln.
    1. Presidents—United States—Biography—Juvenile
literature.    2. Washington, George, 1732-1799—Juvenile
literature.    3. Lincoln, Abraham, 1809-1865—Juvenile
literature.    [1. Washington, George, 1732-1799.
2. Lincoln, Abraham, 1809-1865.    3. Presidents]
I. Halverson, Lydia, ill.    II. Child's World (Firm)
III. Title.
E176.8.F49    1987        973.4'1'0924 [B] [92]        87-10309
ISBN 0-516-02910-X

MY FIRST

# PRESIDENTS' DAY BOOK

# Young George

What kind of boy was Washington?
He liked to swim, and run,
and catch a fish, and ride a horse,
and read when day was done.

He made his brothers wooden swords,
and played at war for fun,
and no one dreamed he'd fight some day
as General Washington.

# The Schoolboy

He wished to be a gentleman,
this boy of long ago,
and so he copied all the rules
that gentlemen should know.

"Sit not when others stand."
"Sleep not when others speak."
He copied off a hundred rules
in less than half a week.

He thought of other rules as well,
like "Duty never shirk."
And then he had a further task:
to put the rules to work!

# Mount Vernon

"I like a farm," said Washington,
"Mount Vernon most of all.
I like to ride my horse and watch
the crops grow green and tall."
And yet he left the place he loved
to meet his country's call.

# Portrait

A tall man, a strong man,
a man upon a horse,
a gentleman in satin coat
and powdered wig, of course.

A three-cornered-hat man
with a uniform for war:
General George Washington
was all of that — and more.

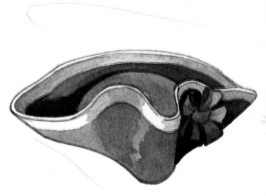

# Valley Forge

At Valley Forge the army camped
in freezing winter weather.
The men were hungry, and their clothes
would hardly hold together.

The General's birthday was at hand.
He wanted one thing only:
help for all his weary men
away from home, and lonely.

Then Martha showed the socks she'd knit
for soldiers of all sizes,
and corn arrived for johnnycake—
a birthday of surprises!

# President Washington

Folks wanted him to be their king,
the war with England won.
He would not hear of such a thing.
He said, "My job is done.
I have no wish for kingly fame,
at *home* I'll be content."
But with some urging, he became
our first great President.

# Washington Monument

High above the town it soars,
five hundred feet and more,
made of marble, gleaming white,
it shines through peace and war.
A fitting way to honor one
who filled his country's needs —
a monument for Washington,
so tall in thoughts and deeds.

# One~Room Cabin

A simple cabin made of logs
was all the Lincolns had . . .
one room, one window and a door,
a loft, and earth that made a floor,
when Abe was just a lad.

And no one, *no one*, ever thought
a humble home like that
would house a future President
who wore a stovepipe hat.

# At Pigeon Creek

He had to sleep
on a corn-husk bed,
because he had no other.
He had to walk
a good long way
for water for his mother.

His hands grew hard
from holding tight
the axe's heavy handle.
He had to read
by fireplace light
because he had no candle.

# A Learnin' Boy

Abe's father called him "lazy."
Abe's second-mother said,
"Lazy? Just you wait and see.
He has a learnin' head."

Abe studied law and thought about
events that came and went,
and Mrs. Lincoln lived to see
that learnin' boy grow up to be
our sixteenth President.

# Growing Tall

Abe Lincoln was a growing lad
those years at Pigeon Creek.
He kept outgrowing sleeves and socks;
it seemed like—every week!

He grew as tall as 6-feet-4,
and it is good to tell
that as he stretched out more and more,
his mind grew tall as well.

# Who?

Who grew up poor,
as a barefoot lad,
and read a book
every chance he had?

Who studied law?
Who stood up tall
and spoke of liberty
for all?

Who wore a shawl
and a tall top hat?
Abraham Lincoln
did all of that!

# Address at Gettysburg

The day was cold, the setting bleak.
The crowd around the speakers' stand
watched Lincoln as he rose to speak,
two sheets of paper in his hand.

The North and South were still at war
when Lincoln spoke with pride
of men who fought at Gettysburg
for freedom's cause, and died.

"Our people must be one," he said.
"Some now are slaves, some free.
*One* nation, under God," he said,
"is what we're meant to be."

# Lincoln Memorial

If you go to Washington,
to Washington, D.C.,
be sure to see the monument
in Lincoln's memory.

You'll see him sitting, thinking,
with wisdom in his face
and charity for everyone
of every faith and race.